Fishing in Rose-Colored Glasses

Jenny Knust

PublishAmerica
Baltimore

© 2010 by Jenny Knust.
All rights reserved. No part of this book may be reproduced, stored in a retrieval system or transmitted in any form or by any means without the prior written permission of the publishers, except by a reviewer who may quote brief passages in a review to be printed in a newspaper, magazine or journal.

First printing

PublishAmerica has allowed this work to remain exactly as the author intended, verbatim, without editorial input.

ISBN: 978-1-4489-6416-1
PUBLISHED BY PUBLISHAMERICA, LLLP
www.publishamerica.com
Baltimore

Printed in the United States of America

Riding on the Rim

I married my husband when I was just out of high school and, though I had a good government job, I had no ambition greater than to be a mother. I knew from the time I was a very little girl that I wanted to have a lot of kids. After I had been married a year, I mentioned to my doctor at my annual exam that I was disappointed I wasn't pregnant yet. Since I was young, he told me to give it another year and then he would consider running some tests. I gave it another year and still no baby. My older sister had a child, and the sister just younger than me had one child and another on the way. I was getting very anxious to start a family.

At my two-year check, my doctor advised me that they would test my husband first, since it's much easier to determine if a man is fertile than a woman. I wish he would have told me that at the one-year check, because it took almost another whole year to convince my husband to give up a manly sample for testing. I've never seen anyone so relieved to be declared "normal." Then it was my turn. The testing, though sometimes grueling and painful, was worth it, because I would have no peace in my life until I had a diagnosis, or preferably a baby. After several months of doctoring and a trip to the immunoinfertility andrology lab at the University of Michigan, I finally got a diagnosis. My gynecologist referred me to a fertility specialist for treatment of my "sperm antibody." Apparently my body recognized my husband's sperm as a foreign object and set out to kill it before it could make the journey nature intended. (A good friend kidded me that this was taking man-hating to the extreme.)

The fertility specialist informed me that there really was no sure treatment for sperm antibody. The chances that I would conceive were about 50 percent, whether I received treatment or not. The first treatment consisted of a regimen of Robitussin cough syrup, followed by a pregnancy test to make sure I wasn't pregnant, then on to a short high-dose course of steroids. Doctors believed the cough syrup worked by thinning the cervical mucus, just as it does the bronchial mucus, giving the sperm a fighting chance to get through.

I took the Robitussin cough syrup, then reported to the lab to give blood for a pregnancy test. The test was negative, and I filled the prescription for steroids and began the second phase of treatment. At the end of the course of steroids, I did not get my period. I was working at a hospital and pulled the physician's desk reference to see what the side effects of the medicine might be. Irregular menstrual cycles. Great! The only thing I could ever really count on was my regular cycles. I called the doctor's office and told the nurse that I was 10 days late. She said, "You better come in for a pregnancy test just to be sure." What a waste of time. I had already had one negative pregnancy test. One more reason to poke me. One more piece of disappointing news. The lab tech told me the nurse should call me with results that afternoon.

I was sitting at my desk when the call came through. I knew better than to get my hopes up. I told myself this would just be another bump on the road to motherhood.

The nurse identified herself and said, "I just called to tell you that your test was positive."

"Positive for what?" I asked, with all sincerity. For a brief moment, I thought I probably tested positive for cancer or some other sort of terrible disease. "It was a pregnancy test, Jenny. A positive result means you are pregnant."

I have never had such a feeling of absolute euphoria. I immediately called my husband and told him the good news. I was so looking forward to talking about it with him in person. I hopped in my 82 Mustang and headed for home. I was on cloud nine the entire half-hour drive. I could not wait to get home and see the look on my husband's face. I beat him home and waited anxiously in the kitchen. When he walked through the door, I was standing there, about to confirm the happiest news of my life. Before I could speak, he said, "Jenny, how long did you drive on the flat tire?"

"I didn't have a flat tire," I said indignantly, wondering why this special announcement had to be muddied by tire talk.

"The tire is completely gone, and the wheel dug a rut all the way up the driveway."

I've ruined a few more tires along the way, but none has ever been sacrificed for such a worthy cause. Motherhood has turned out to be just as wonderful as I dreamed it would be, and I am thankful every day for God's gracious generosity toward me. The day before the pregnancy test, I had offered a prayer of thanksgiving and promised God I would be thankful for all my blessings and accept his plan for me, no matter how the test turned out.

Simple truth: Sometimes God just wants us to acknowledge the blessings we have before he heaps more on.

An Extreme, Divine Intervention

M**any a busy woman** has ended the day with a prayer of thanksgiving just for the strength to make it through the day. We know that we can't do all that needs to be done without God's daily injections of strength, encouragement and energy.

The most undeniably spectacular case of divine intervention in my life came in the form of a phone call. One cold 1980s evening, I received a call at bedtime from my husband's sister, who was at that time a junior in college. She was sobbing almost hysterically as she announced that she had been to the doctor earlier in the day and found out she was pregnant. She was intending to marry her long-time boyfriend when she graduated from college, but a wedding was hardly even on the radar.

We held a 30-minute phone conversation, during which I consoled her and assured her that I would do anything I could to help, including babysitting free of charge if need be. I was home with two little ones and would have no problem taking care of another. She believed her conservative parents would never understand or accept the pregnancy. I told her that her father would probably be grouchy for awhile and her mother would have to make a trip to the bathroom. (Grammy suffered from some sort of strange syndrome that caused her to have an immediate case of diarrhea when she heard bad news). But I was sure they would love the child just as much as they did mine. The only thing I was not willing to do was tell her parents about the pregnancy, which she had begged me to do. I believed with all my heart that news like that, even though painful to deliver, should come from the source.

I thought I was successful in putting at least a few of her fears to rest and hung up the phone. The phone rang within 30 seconds. I assumed there was something my sister-in-law had forgotten to tell me. It was my mother-in-law on the line. Before I tell "the rest of the story," it is important to note that, when we first built a house down the road from my in-laws, we had party phone lines. About nine families shared one phone line, making it almost impossible to get the phone when you wanted it. About two years earlier, when the phone company offered private lines, all nine families eagerly accepted the rate increase in exchange for privacy.

The voice on the other end of phone announced, "Jenny, this is Mom. Something is wrong with our phone lines. I picked the phone up to call a friend, and I could hear everything you and Sarah were saying. Dad is yelling in the bedroom, and I had to go to the bathroom." And all I could think about was that I had talked about her bathroom problem not knowing she was on the line. Thankfully the rest of the points made about Grammy were flattering.

I immediately called my sister-in-law back and said, "I don't know if anyone but you is listening, but your mom called, and she just heard every word we said." Her response: "Thank God. Now I don't have to tell them."

We have talked about that incident many times in the last 20 years. There is no explanation for it. The phone lines had never been crossed before, nor have they been crossed since. We both still believe it is a clear cut case of divine intervention. I love the saying, "God never gives you more than you can handle." I believe, in a most spectacular fashion, he spared my sister-in-law from the agony of a confession that she could not bear to make in person. And both of us have learned to not take privacy for granted.

The simple truth: God can and does work miracles every day, usually when we have not even thought to ask.

Tough Love

When we have children, we know that we love them with all our heart, but sometimes we wonder if they love us as much as we do them. I never doubted for a second that my daughter loved me. She was my firstborn, and I quit work to stay home and take care of her. We spent countless hours puttering, walking up the hill to visit Grandma & Grandpa, and frittering the days away reading books and playing Barbie. She was attached to her daddy, but there was no doubt she was a mama's girl.

When my son came along two and a half years later, it was not as obvious to me that he loved me as much as I loved him. He was all boy—big for his age from the day he was born and obsessed with boy things like cars and tractors. He loved to go to the farm with his dad and one of his first phrases was "Grandpa's boy" (taught by Grandpa, of course). He was a man's man, even when he was a baby boy.

One day, in a misguided attempt to measure my son's love, I hatched a plan to see what he would do if I dropped dead of some sort of medical condition. I was pretty sure he would miss me terribly and realize how much he loved me if I was dead. I lay motionless on the living room floor as he toddled over to me to see what was up. He shook me a bit and said, "Mommy, mommy." I stayed in character.

As I heard the pitter patter of little boy feet, I cracked one eye open and watched him run away. What could he be doing? I knew he was too young to use the phone. Maybe he was going to find sissy to help with the pseudo-crisis.

As I watched from the corner of one eye, I saw him pick up a toy and come running back to my motionless body. I shut my eye and waited for his next move. And then he laid it on me. He showed his love and concern for me by whacking me across the bridge of the nose with a matchbox car. It worked. Mommy instantly came back to life, tear-filled eyes wide open. He seemed pleased at my resurrection. I felt like an absolute fool, wearing around a big scab between my eyes for the next two weeks. And I couldn't even be one bit mad, because after all, it was a clear-cut case of entrapment.

My daughter was much more affectionate than my son. He rarely sought me out for comfort or affection. I considered it a rare treat when he would climb up on my lap for snuggling. One day he crawled up on my lap, and as he looked into my eyes, I said to myself, "Ohhh, he does love me." Just about that time, he reached one little hand up toward my face and in one smooth motion, he quickly took a chunk out of my lower lip with the fingernail clippers. I think it was payback for the "mommy pretends to be dead" incident. And the scab on my lip was just as pretty and lasted just as long as the scab on my nose. He's all grown up, but I still like to show him the scar on mommy's lip from the clipper incident. I've since just chosen to assume that my son loves me, as assuming the opposite has just brought me pain and suffering.

Simple truth: Testing the love of another person rarely gets the expected result and usually ends up being a very painful experience.

Bringing Home the Bacon

My friends and I have spent countless hours pondering the plight of the modern woman. We have financial freedom our mothers never had, but we have ten times the responsibility. Forty years ago, women were totally dependent upon their husbands and many of them felt trapped because they had no ability to make a living for themselves. Somewhere along the line, society told women that there was more important work to be done than taking care of a home and family.

So now we get to run with the rats by day and take care of a home and family by night.

I stayed at home with my kids when they were little because I wanted to get them off to a good start in life. I wanted them to sleep as long as they wanted to in the morning and have a leisurely breakfast that was not followed by bundling up and heading off to daycare. I didn't want to ever have to ponder whether I should go to work or stay home with sick children. There are some decisions a mother just shouldn't have to make.

I went back to work just before my youngest turned five, and only then because my sister offered to watch him. She was home alone with her youngest son, and the two boys were best buddies. Our sons would play the day away while my sister studied for her evening college classes. If her husband had to work overtime, I would pick up my kids after work and take hers home with me and feed them dinner. They liked to eat at Aunt Jenny's house, because farmers always have better cuts of meat than city folks. There were days when my son would have preferred to stay home, but once he got there, he could easily be engaged in the little boy daily activities.

When I was home with my kids, I wanted for nothing. My husband had a job that paid a modest wage and he also worked on the family farm. He had an old pickup, and I drove a very average car. I had three pairs of jeans, two or three nice sweatshirts, a few church dresses, and one drawer full of sweatpants and t-shirts. Though money was tight, I never felt deprived, and we seemed to always find a way to afford upgrades to the house and small family vacations. In all the jobs I've had since, I have never felt the kind of contentment and satisfaction that I did taking care of my children.

After I went back to work, I convinced myself that I needed a new wardrobe about every six months. I spent a good share of my salary on clothes and shoes, but always felt justified because, after all, I needed to look good to get the next good job that came open. The better the job, the more clothes I needed. It took me years to realize that I was just buying clothes as a reward that could not be found in my work.

A very wise friend once told me she thought the whole women's movement that sent us out into the work world in droves really started with a perfume commercial where the model in a beautiful gown sang the virtues of being able to bring home the bacon and fry it up in the pan, while never ever letting you "forget you're a man." I told her there were days when I was so tired and grouchy after bringing home the bacon and frying it up in the pan that I wanted to sling hot grease all over the kitchen and light it on fire. That's what happens when we try to do to much. The joys and rewards that should come of giving of ourselves turn into resentment and bitterness about having to do it all.

Simple truth: We must find a way to appreciate all that we have, without feeling that we have to do it all.

Smell no Evil

My daughter once sent me an e-mail with the subject line, "See, Mama, you were right." The web link attached lead me to a research article on the internet, entitled, "Sensitivity to Odors may be Linked to Fertility, Sex Hormones." Now, before you go thinking bad thoughts about me or my daughter, you should know that the gist of the article, published in *Nature Neuroscience*, was that women in childbearing years are able to detect certain odors in surprisingly small doses. The researcher speculated that this heightened sense of smell in the fertile years may have helped our ancestral mothers:

> forage for food;
> recognize kin;
> select mates; and
> bond with children.

The summer my son was five and my daughter was seven, a bird built its home in the furnace flue. My husband removed the nest, but still I could hear rummaging, scratching, and peeping in the furnace room. And I detected the subtle yet distinct odor of propane. Although my husband insisted that the nest was gone and the smell of propane was present only in my imagination, he begrudgingly went back to the roof. He sent a golf ball down the flue, which rolled out of the furnace without nesting materials. He once again declared the flue to be clear. The peeping and gas smell continued until the day a full-grown bird flew out of the furnace and terrorized the household. Perhaps mother was smelling gas after all. "Maybe we should call the furnace guy," my husband suggested nonchalantly.

Our long-time furnace repairman could only come on one of the two days a week that I worked. What he didn't know when he took the call is that he was about to be treated to the best little repairman's helper in the world. Many a plumber and carpenter had tried to shake little Ted, who hung tight and questioned even the slightest move. My daughter called me at work to report the furnace repairman's findings.

"Mom, Earl was here and Ted went downstairs with him to the furnace room. Ted told him, "My mom says she smells gas, but my dad says she's crazy.' Earl's gas detector started beeping, and Earl told Ted, 'I don't know if your mom's crazy or not, but she does smell gas.' You were right, Mama." I hung up the phone and did the happy dance for my co-workers, who had followed the bird's nest/propane saga with great concern.

I couldn't help but wonder how much further that researcher could have gone. Could he have proven that only women in their childbearing years are able to smell a rotten potato in the cupboard? Or what about a child in need of a diaper change? Maybe only women of childbearing age can smell the dog's latest accident, the body odor of the last person to sit in her rollercoaster seat, or a sour dishrag in the sink upon return from vacation.

And what if the researcher had tested the other senses? I bet he might have found that women of childbearing age can see things that others can't. I think these items might include dirty socks, cobwebs in the corner, empty pop cans or candy wrappers on the floor. And what about the sense of hearing? I think only a woman of childbearing age can hear the dog rustling in an empty water bowl, a teen-aged boy rustling outside her daughter's window or the chirp of a smoke detector needing a new battery. I'm pretty sure that women in other age groups and all men cannot hear any of these things, or surely they would be compelled to take some sort of corrective action.

But, alas, I've been accused on some occasions of seeing and hearing things that others don't. There are medicines that help with that, I suppose, but I like to stay on guard so that I can forage for food (i.e., pop and potato chips), recognize kin (i.e., teen-aged children with ever-changing hair colors), and bond with my children (despite their endless efforts to push me away). I married young, so I'm hoping my underdeveloped sense of smell didn't cause me to select the wrong mate. I've been married 30 years, so I guess my immature sense of smell must have served me pretty well, even though my mate doesn't seem to know the smell of propane from a hole in the ground.

Simple truth: Nobody can be right all of the time. Disregarding the opinions of others is always risky business.

Finding (and Destroying) the Ugly Button

Most of the time, I would describe myself as pretty good-natured. Like everyone else, I have my buttons—things that can change me from Mrs. Hyde to Dr. Jekyll almost instantly.

If there's one thing that pushes my ugly button above all others, it's searching for something I just had in my hands a few minutes earlier. I'm sure I'm not the only woman alive who has frantically searched through a stack of papers on her desk, while a boss or co-worker waits impatiently for her to produce the all-important document. I've destroyed garments I have painstakingly constructed with a scissor snip gone awry because I could not find my fifty-cent seam ripper. I've thrown away little plastic pieces and parts that have laid around for weeks, only to find out the next day that the little piece held something very important together. I once searched for a magazine for a week, only to find it under a pile of clothing on the ironing board.

On some occasions, I have been foolish enough to enlist the assistance of family members in my ill-fated hide and seek missions. Their inability to immediately produce the missing prize only fuels my fury. I can vividly remember a fit of frustration during which taught my son how to properly search. "Tip your head down to the ground. Now look at eye level. Now tilt your head up. Look from side to side." I don't know if the mental image of myself actually turning his head from side to side for him is a dark piece of family history or just a recurring daydream.

My behavior while searching for something is so notoriously ugly that I have heard my kids mutter to each other, "Oh, no. She's looking for something. Let's get out of here!" In order to maintain health and happiness, I have tried very hard to get organized. Plastic containers are great for organizing clutter. Color-coded file folders help me keep things organized at work. I have tried to make a conscious effort to make a mental note of where I am laying things down, or better yet, put them away where they belong. For the sake of my gradually rising blood pressure, and because it pains me to hear my children refer to me as a "nut," I have learned to let it go for today if I can. Things turn up in due time, though sometimes it's after you've bought a replacement.

In this hectic and stressful life we live in, it is important to avoid the things that cause us grief, unhappiness or unmitigated anger. We should take time to dissect the problems that cause us the greatest amount of stress, whether it's something as simple as a filing system or as complex as a relationship with a family member. Life is too short to allow ugliness to creep in and affect our happiness, even for just a few minutes.

When my children reflect on the mother that raised them, I hope they remember Mother Hyde at the kitchen table, decorating sugar cookies with a smile on her face, not Mother Jekyll, with her head under the couch muttering obscenities.

Simple truth: Most of the chaos in our lives is self-inflicted because we fail to take time to solve the small problems.

High on Life

It has always seemed to me that some people are just born happy. I believe I am one of those people. When I talk about how joyful life can be, my son likes to sing (in his old lady voice), "I've got the joy, joy, joy, joy down in my heart," as he swings his imaginary jug of Granny Clampett's moonshine. I can honestly admit that I have never had a moonshine-induced moment of happiness. All of them have been the real thing.

When I was in my mid thirties, I took a psychology class at a local community college. I was in a room full of twenty-somethings, who spent a good deal of time talking about last night's party. When we began to study the chapter on intoxication, they found a whole new interest in a class that had previously bored them to tears. They began telling tales about what kind of "drunk" they were. Some were mean drunks and some were sad drunks. Some were vomit-in-your-friend's-car drunks, and some admitted to drinking to the point of passing out. I sat quietly, having no drunken stories of my own to tell.

Because I usually had an opinion on most every topic discussed in class, they finally realized that I had not said a word. One of the young things sitting next to me asked, "What kind of drunk are you?" I said, "I don't know. I've never been drunk." You could have heard a pin drop on a feather pillow. All heads turned toward the old lady in the middle of the room. One rather hardened welfare mother said to me in a most serious voice, "What do you take?" Surely if I hadn't ever been drunk, I must be popping or snorting something stronger. I don't know that I ever really convinced them that I had never been under the influence. (I didn't tell them about the time I was given Valium before surgery and later didn't remember telling everyone in the room what I got them for Christmas).

As the class progressed, the professor began to describe the signs of intoxication. I was fascinated to learn that people who are drunk lose track of time, have trouble concentrating on what others are saying to them, and have a sense of euphoria. And then it hit me. I have been drunk. I have those same symptoms when I'm working on my scrapbooks! Hours go by. I don't hear my husband rummaging for supper, and I am absolutely ecstatic about the beautiful page I just pulled together.

It's hard for most people to understand when you tell them you don't need alcohol. For me it comes down to self-control. If I make a fool out of myself, I want to remember every single detail and try not to repeat the same mistake. If somebody says to me, "Do you remember dancing naked on the table last night?", I want to be able to say, "Yes, I'm sorry you had to see that, and I'll never do that again."

Simple truth: Finding simple pleasures that bring joy is much less harmful to the body (and soul) than drugs or alcohol.

Always Wear Clean Underwear

When you hear people reciting motherly advice, it almost always includes the "always wear clean underwear in case you're in a wreck," nugget of wisdom. I often wear my legs unshaven for several weeks during the winter. I'm not very hairy anyway, my skin is dry, and I don't plan on being in a wreck. When I do shave, it's not the thought that my husband may be repulsed by my hairy legs that compels me to do so, but the thought of ending up in the hospital with hairy legs. A different twist on the old clean underwear theme.

When I was in eighth grade, I collided head to head with another girl in early morning basketball practice. I was guarding a girl as she dribbled up the floor, and another set of dribblers was coming our way. The back of our heads cracked together somewhere around the center line. I managed to get showered and get to class, despite the three-inch goose egg on the back of my head.

The accident happened on a Friday, and junior high basketball games were on Saturday morning. On the day before the game, the girls wore dresses, and the boys wore ties. I had a lovely pink and purple dress, accessorized by some pink panty hose, a very fetching getup in the 70's. I had worn those pink pantyhose before, so I knew they were the kind with the crotch that drifts further and further down as the day goes on. This was back in the days when panty hose did not have built in crotches. So, in order to solve the creeping crotch dilemma, I had put on one pair of underwear, then my pink pantyhose, then another pair of underwear to hold up the pantyhose. It was rather hot, but, hey, it was better than pantyhose crotch at my knees.

About a half hour into the first class, I began to see orange stars, and it sounded like the teacher's voice was coming from a tin can. The intense headache set in, and I was lucky enough to get to the bathroom before the vomiting commenced. The school secretary called my mom to come get me, as they could tell that I had apparently sustained more than a minor injury. My mom showed up with the vomit bucket in hand and took me to the local clinic. The medical student came in with the doctor and looked me over. They were quite sure I had suffered a concussion and was now experiencing a migraine headache. My mother gave them the okay to give me a shot to control the pain. Of course this was a shot that had to be given in the hip. Imagine the surprise in the room as they peeled off layer after layer of underwear and pantyhose. I was too sick to care, but my mom and I laughed about it later. I think she was proud of me though. I not only had on clean underwear, but pink pantyhose and another pair of clean underwear to spare. Talk about covering all your bases (and all your girl parts too!).

Simple truth: Mothers are usually on the right track and looking out for our best interests. Life would be much simpler if we heeded their advice more and second-guessed them less.

Waiting in the Wings

Have you ever known a child who seemed to behave for everyone except his or her parents? My husband has such a nephew, who luckily outgrew the tendency to hurl insults and sling mud every time he was told to do something by his mother or father. But cousin Wil always behaved for Uncle Tony, mainly because when Cousin Wil was good, Uncle Tony would take him to the farm.

Wil had learned to read the signs when a trip to the farm was about to occur, and he would stick tighter and tighter as Uncle Tony put on his boots and coats and began searching for a cap. He was so determined to go along that Uncle Tony found it easier to take him than shake him. Occasionally there was just too much work to be done to have a toddler underfoot. As Uncle Tony tried to go through the pre-farm trip motions in a low-key manner, so as not to arouse any interest, Wil began to suspect something was in the works. "Where you going Uncle Tony?" He asked twice before he got an answer. "To Rome, to see the Pope," responded Uncle Tony (which made the adult Lutherans in the house chuckle quietly). Without missing a beat, Cousin Wil responded, "Is the Pope at the farm?"

One summer day Wil accompanied Uncle Tony to the farm to watch him work on the tractor. Because a tractor on blocks can be unpredictably dangerous, Cousin Wil was asked to sit on a chair in the corner of the shop while the repair work began. Uncle Tony was usually pretty patient about playing the one thousand questions about farming game, but today the stress of a difficult repair caused him to ask Cousin Wil to sit as quietly as he could until the work was done. He squirmed in his seat and tried to honor the request for about all of one minute. Finally, being unable to hold his thoughts in any longer, he popped the all-important question: "Uncle Tony, if that tractor falls on you, can I have your motorcycle?"

We have laughed many times at what could have been a simple request, had it not been that Uncle Tony had a son who would probably be in line for the motorcycle if the tractor repair had gone awry. But I guess it didn't hurt to ask. A guy's got to keep on top of things if he's going to get ahead on the farm.

Simple truth: Every one of us has the opportunity to positively impact the life of a child by giving of our love, talent and most importantly our time.

Beware of Friends' Prayers

I am a firm believer in the power of prayer. I have seen people who were not supposed to live pull through with flying colors, and I have seen people come to grips with a demon they were wrestling because others offered up their love and concerns in prayer.

A few years ago, I was involved in a hideous employment situation. I was the director of a floundering senior campus. The property had been plagued by years of mismanagement, and many of the residents had been duped out of their life savings by unscrupulous people and business practices. The new owner convinced me that his company was prepared to provide whatever resources were necessary to turn the property around, a promise which turned out to be quite empty.

The first year went fairly well, and I felt like I had realized a minor victory in my efforts to restore trust with staff and residents. A consultant who had done some work for the new company during the initial takeover, and whom I had known for quite sometime, tried to warn me what I was getting into. He said, "Here's how it's going to go, Jenny. The first year is going to be fine. You'll be allowed a great deal of flexibility and resources to try to accomplish what you think needs to be done. At the one year mark, the owners are going to open up the books and see how badly they are bleeding. At that point, the hammer will come down. If they like you, you might buy another six months. If they don't, you'll be out the door." His words could not have been more prophetic.

At exactly the one-year mark, I became involved in a game of treachery and deceit, perpetrated by two employees, one who worked for the company on the construction side of the business, and one who worked directly under me. Both individuals were fabricating stories and exaggerating situations to make the owner understand how incapable I was of managing the property. I did not realize the depth of the deception until it was too late.

A Thursday afternoon conference call that included me and the employee directly under me who had been reporting falsehoods behind my back resulted in my being issued a laundry list of dirty deeds, which included firing hard-working, fragile employees who had fallen out of favor with the construction guy and the other employee. I sat crying silently throughout the conference call. In the next 48 hours, there were conversations and political maneuvers the likes of which have not been seen since Watergate.

When the day began, I had voiced a sense of impending doom to another lady who worked for me. She and I had become great friends, and she had suspected and tried to warn me that there were treacherous games being played behind my back. Before the conference call, I had prayed quietly to myself all day, "God, please just let this be a peaceful conversation." When it was all over and the depth of the treachery had been exposed, I knew my dream job was gone. Baffled as to why my prayer for peace was apparently not heard, I met the employee in the hall and confessed my frustration as to why God did not answer my prayer for peace. She said, "Jenny, I have been praying all day that the evil that is working against you would be exposed."

Looking back at the end of the day, I remembered a conversation I had with a visiting pastor in the hallway. He was a kind, gentle man who knew that there were some troubles. When he had asked earlier if there was anything I could do, I told him, "Say a little prayer for us. I think the devil is in the building." He told me, "I'm going to pray that you will clearly see how the devil is working against you." The next time I saw him, we had a laugh about how the two prayers for exposure had apparently trumped the prayer for peace. In the end, I lost the battle with the devil, but I haven't given up the war. For the prayers of friends are more powerful than the devil. But it might help to know just what they're asking God for on your behalf before you get your heart set on something else.

Simple truth: The prayer of a righteous man availeth much, but maybe not as much as a couple of his well-meaning friends.

Unconditional Grammy Love

My mother-in-law was one of the most awesome, fun people I've ever known. We did not have the typical mother-in-law and daughter-in-law relationship. People used to be mortified when I would tell them I was taking a few days off work to vacation with my mother-in-law. They had never heard of such, and this situation would prompt them to break in to a tirade about how unpleasant they found their mother-in-law.

She was just past 50 years of age when she finally became a Grandma. The oldest daughter did not want children, and the youngest was still in college. My husband and I had tried for several years before finally producing the first grandchild. Our daughter was the apple of Grammy's eye, but she loved the next three just as much.

One day my sister was babysitting for my son, and they stumbled on his Grammy in the aisle at the grocery store. "You better go say hello to your Grandma," my sister advised. Ted took off down the aisle, and when he got to Grammy, he put a bear hug on her leg. Grammy stood almost six feet tall, so there was plenty of leg to latch on to.

My sister watched in amazement as my mother-in-law continued her conversation with an acquaintance in the grocery store aisle, all the while patting young Ted lovingly on the back. When she finally took a breath from her conversation, she looked down in total surprise and said, "Well, Ted, Grandma didn't see you there." Who she thought might be yanking at her leg we'll never know, but the message was clear—any youngster would be welcome to give Grammy a hug, anywhere, anytime.

If there were only more people like Grammy, who are comfortable showing love and affection even to a stranger (who just happens to turn out to be a grandson), wouldn't the world be a better place to live?

Simple truth: Jesus said it best when he said, "Let the children come unto me, for such is the kingdom of God."

Living in the Fog of Self-Pity

I've wasted very few of the days given to me on self-pity, although I must admit that I have been richly blessed and have had very little grief or sorrow in my life. To me, self-pity is a most useless and unproductive endeavor.

Two of my sisters and I took a vacation together one summer. We bought cheap tickets online, which turned an average length trip into a three-leg journey. A few times two of us were seated together but not all three. We would meet up at the next airport and discuss any details we had dragged out of the passengers sitting next to us. We are all incredibly nosy, so this would fill what little time we had during layovers.

On the way home, I was separated from the sisters on all three legs of the journey. The first leg wasn't too lonely, because I was finishing up a book, and they were both seated alone. On the second leg of the trip, they got to sit together, a few rows in front of me. If I peeked over the seats, I could sometimes see them chatting away. To make matters worse, I was seated in the middle seat, between two 40-something men who were apparently traveling together, although the guy to my left fell asleep almost immediately after boarding. The guy to the right said hello, then promptly put on his headphones. Any flier knows that the headphones are a universal sign for "I don't really want to get to know you." I sat sandwiched between these two non-communicative strangers, wishing I was sitting with my sisters.

As the plane was beginning to descend into Minneapolis, the guy on my right took off his earphones and asked where I was headed. I told him Des Moines and asked him the same. He explained that he was catching a bus to an army base in Wisconsin. He looked more like a surfer dude than an army guy, so I asked, "What are you doing at an Army base?" He replied, "I play in a band."

"Is it a band I might know?" I asked. He looked me in the eye, paused momentarily (for effect or maybe to try to guess whether I was old enough to know), and responded, "Foghat."

"Foghat," I squealed, like a teenaged girl. He seemed pleased. I rattled off a few of the 70's songs I remembered, and he gave me a brief summary of how he ended up in the band. When the conversation was finished, he pulled a photograph of the band from his bag and signed it for me.

You can bet I won the "who had the most interesting passenger in the next seat" contest for the entire trip. And as the sisters and I hopped on a golf cart to catch the next leg, they were pretty impressed when Foghat's Charlie waved goodbye to me and the sisters. I was so angry at myself for not trying to strike up a conversation sooner. But, alas, I was lost in a self-pitying fog, watching enviously as the sisters chattered away.

I try not to pester people when they can't get away from me, but if they open up even a small crack in the door, they better be prepared to tell their life story.

Simple truth: One of life's greatest blessings can be found in being open to meeting new people. Why bury your head in a book when God places colorful characters all around us?

Traveling with a Misanthrope

Most people would probably think that I have a pretty good command of the English language (my math aptitude is not open for discussion). I like to learn new words and enjoy the challenge of spinning them into a phrase that will get me a good laugh, or a cry, or just any kind of reaction at all.

My kids and I used to play a dictionary game with my sister and her kids when we visited. The object of the game is to choose a word from the dictionary that nobody at the table knows. Points are scored by getting your tablemates to choose your fictitious definition. I am so profoundly competitive that I began to study for this game, searching for new words and eloquent definitions with which to trick the stiff competition. My son found one of my study lists and asked, "What kind of dork studies for the dictionary game?" I let his snide comment go, because I knew he was bitter because his mother always stands on the imaginary winner's podium at the end of the game.

I was sent to Florida on business and took my son and daughter with me. They were older teenagers at the time. We caught a few of the Disney parks in Orlando. As we maneuvered through the crowds, my daughter seemed to grow more and more irritable. She finally stopped in the middle of the street, threw her hands up in the air, and with tears in her eyes, asked, "Why do I always have to move over when I meet someone?" She was feeling every bit of her five foot three inch stature as we moved through crowds that seemed to tower over her. Her brother, who stands well over six feet tall, had no idea what she was talking about.

In her tearful state, my daughter described how "all of her life" she had been forced to move over when she meets someone on the street. "Why can't other people move over for me once in awhile?" she lamented. I made a conscious effort to see if her accusations were founded. I must admit that she did seem to get pushed aside by oncoming traffic. As the next person drove her off the sidewalk, I tried to minimize the situation. She snapped back, "Mother, you are going to have to face it. I am a misanthrope." A misanthrope? "What in the world is that?" I asked. My son seemed amused that the queen of the dictionary game was stumped. "Mis, as in not or doesn't," my daughter responded. "Anthrope, as in the science of man." When we got home, I ran for the dictionary and confirmed her definition. There, beside the world "misanthrope," laid the cold hard truth. My daughter is a hater of mankind.

The irony of the situation is that my daughter ended up being a school teacher. This "hater of mankind" tells me that she loves children. She only hates adults. Funny thing is, most kids come complete with a set of parents to be reckoned with. And parents usually come in the form of adults.

My daughter spent the rest of the day at the Disney park seeing how many people she could force off the sidewalk by holding her ground. In retrospect, I'm not sure which was the more disheartening revelation—the fact that I had raised a misanthrope, a "hater of mankind," or that it was one less word to be used in my endless quest to dominate the dictionary game.

Simple truth: Life would be much better for all if we gave up our spot on the sidewalk for another.

Buck & Mary's Hired Man

Most teenaged boys seem to spend quite a bit of time playing video games and engaging in other rather sedentary endeavors. My son Ted was never the sit-around-the-house sort. He liked to stay busy and didn't mind hard work. When his guidance counselor recommended him to an elderly couple looking for a boy with a "strong back" to do some yard work, Ted eagerly accepted the position.

The teenaged Ted was not particularly chatty, and I wondered what he would have to talk about with Buck and Mary. I knew Mary would fix him some lunch, and I had a mental picture of Ted sitting with people he barely knew, at a loss for words and feeling uncomfortable. When he arrived home, I asked what they talked about, and with a disgust in his voice I had come to expect, he advised me that he and Buck talked about World War II, and the three of them engaged in a lively discussion about skunks. I felt silly for having asked the question.

Buck and Mary's son, who is the athletic director at a community college, asked his parents if they would like to come down to watch a football game. They respectfully declined, advising him that they were going to Ted's game. We laughed with their son about the bond that was forming between Buck and Mary and their new hired man.

When the U.S. census was distributed that fall, we were lucky enough to receive the full survey form, all twenty-some pages. There were specific questions to be answered regarding the employment status of each member of the household. My husband and I completed our sections begrudgingly, and when Ted asked if he could fill out his own employment section, we tossed better judgment aside and let him do his thing. It went something like this:

Q; In the past week, have you been employed? If so, what is the name of your employer?
A: Yes. Buck and Mary.
Q: How would you describe your position?
A: Lawn maintenance
Q: What were your primary duties during the past week?
A: Picking up walnuts.
Q: How long does it take you to get to work?
A: Five minutes if Dad drives; 15 minutes if Buck drives. (Buck is famous for backing up traffic in his old, red pick-up truck.)

We photocopied his responses and shared them with Buck and Mary, who appreciated Ted's sense of humor and lighthearted approach to his important assignments.

Ted has been described as an "old soul." As a teenager, he liked to stop by the co-op after school and play cards with the old farmers. But mostly he has a respect for his elders, which makes him well-liked by people of all ages. And if he likes you back, he might even pick up your walnuts!

Simple truth: There's no expiration date on a sense of humor. The older you get, the more you'll need it!

The Meaning of Life

One of my husband's supervisors, a man who could best be described as an interesting character, recently blindsided him with an unexpected question. "Why is everyone walking around like anything they're doing really matters?" he asked. A Discovery Channel special on the probability of a meteor crashing into Earth had this man, who describes himself as "not particularly religious but not an atheist either," completely unnerved. The realization that earth could be wiped out at any moment had this fellow deep in contemplation about the meaning of life.

My sister-in-law reported that she once discovered the meaning of life. But apparently when the root canal was over and the nitrous oxide wore off, her life returned to the muddled, confused mess she remembered before sitting down in the dentist's chair. With all the bad news these days, a numbing of the senses can sometimes provide the illusion of peace and clarity. People use drugs, alcohol, and a hundred other unhealthy habits to try to escape the realities of the sinful world we live in.

In these days of hectic confusion and almost hopeless uncertainty, it is only natural that people have a heightened curiosity about the meaning of life. Why are we here? What are we supposed to be doing with our lives? Just when we think the answers to these questions will not come in our lifetime, we find ourselves in a moment that brings at least a little peace and clarity of purpose. My son and I experienced such a moment at the funeral of a friend.

My son had developed a bond with Buck and Mary, an older couple that hired him to do yard work. Mary passed away suddenly the day after New Years day. She sat down in the chair in the middle of the night and suffered a fatal heart attack.

Mary almost defies description. At the time of her death, she was a very young 80 years old, with rapier wit and a fantastic sense of humor. But she was most admired for her hospitality. She was a gracious and loving hostess to friends, family, and even strangers. One of Mary's sons eloquently described his mother when he told me, "Mom had a way of dealing with each person that made you think she felt something special for you that she didn't feel for anyone else."

Though my son understood the importance of going to the funeral, he was very uncomfortable with the idea of going to the home after the service. I knew that his presence would be of comfort to the family, as Mary frequently spoke fondly of Ted to family and friends. I watched proudly as my son not only accepted a hug from Mary's daughter but actually hugged back. The best I had been able to do in the hug department for several years prior is to be allowed to wrap my arms around my six-foot, four-inch son while he held his arms stiff at his sides. His sister, aunts and I likened it to hugging a tree. I watched proudly as my son learned a little bit about comfort and a whole lot more about the meaning of life.

Mary's priest comforted a church full of grieving family members and friends with these words: "The Bible tells us there are many mansions in heaven. I have no doubt that Mary is cleaning one of them out right now." Through the tears of grief, we shared a light-hearted moment that Mary would have appreciated. We laughed as we remembered fondly a fun-loving mother, grandmother, and friend, who understood that God, family and friends make life meaningful.

I think that one of life's greatest ironies is that we won't fully comprehend its meaning until it's over. And as the great thinkers, celebrities, famous athletes, and successful business people spend their days in search of the next revelation to help us make sense of life, "ordinary" people, living loving lives and giving generously of their time and talents have already figured it out.

Simple truth: Mary lived 80 precious years on earth and raised a God-loving family, who knows she is in heaven. The meaning of life is just that simple.

Fishin' in My Rose-Colored Glasses

My mom has a theory that some people are just born happy and some are not. I guess I buy that for the most part. And if it is true, I would probably be considered one of those born happy. My parents told me they didn't know a baby could smile so much until I was born.

One of the popular business philosophies touted in the 90s was FISH!, a training series based on the customer service principles employed by the Seattle Fish Market. Buying into the FISH! Philosophy was a no brainer for me. I wouldn't last more than ten minutes in a workplace where people didn't appreciate (and reciprocate) my sick sense of humor.

Until marrying a farmer, I had never witnessed or participated in a chicken butchering session. I went along with it, thanks to an exposé I had seen on how contaminated chicken processing factories are and the deplorable conditions where chickens are processed. Luckily my in-laws were seasoned chicken butchers, so they knew all the slick tricks to quickly remove the craw, crack open the breast bone, and clean out the innards.

There was an elderly lady who, before moving to town and allowing her son to take over the family farm next door, had done her share of chicken butchering. Fern was an incredibly optimistic and upbeat lady. I met up with her in her son's yard, and we shared chicken butchering techniques. I was complaining to her about how disgusting I found the whole process, fully expecting her to commiserate with me. With the sweet little smile that seemed to be permanently etched into her lovely face, she told me, "Oh, I never minded it. Whenever I have a task like that, I just say to myself, 'This isn't really so bad,' and that makes it a lot better." The fellows at the Seattle Fish Market would have been proud of her. I went away chuckling and shaking my head, wondering how I would ever effectively employ such a simplistic mind trick.

My son, Ted, could certainly relate to the Fern attitude. He was an enthusiastic little farmer-in-the-making and insisted on being in the middle of everything farm-related. His older sister went crying to the house after the first axe fell, never to be seen again on chicken butchering day. (She later became a vegetarian and credits the whole chicken killing gig for that decision.)

The men would go down to the chicken house and grab a few victims at a time, dragging them clucking and flopping out to the chopping block. My husband would hold the chicken, and his dad would swing the axe. My mother-in-law and I waited for the slain fowl in the shop up the hill, where we had cutting tables, sharp knives and tubs of cold water. Ted's job was to bring the chickens from the chopping block up the hill to mom and grandma.

With great enthusiasm and vigor, he would make trip after trip, never tiring of his assignment. Toward the end of the day's work, we noticed that he seemed to be singing as he trudged along, dead bird in each hand. As he got closer, we heard the beautiful words of his Fern-like song, set to a tune that would make even the most weary farmer want to dance a little jig. "Grandpa pounds their heads off. Grandma pulls their guts out." That was pretty much the gist of every verse. It certainly lightened the load for Mom & Grandma, as we contemplated how a child could get such a kick out of such a disgusting job. We asked him to never sing that song off the farm, unless he was at Fern's house. She's one of the few people who would have understood and approved.

Simple truth: Bringing a positive attitude to the table (even the butchering table) can make even the most unpleasant task bearable.

Just Another Face in the Crowd

Unless you were born at home, you probably spent your first few days of life in a room full of wrinkled little strangers, whose identities were known only to family members and friends who loved them. My first week of life was spent in this room full of screaming strangers, although I later came to know one of those little red-faced nobodies as my school classmate, Don. Yes, Don and I started our lives together as just another couple of wrinkled little faces in the crowd, dependent upon the care of others.

As we progressed from infancy to childhood, we became increasingly aware of our individuality and so very conscious of our own appearance. A simple red blotch on the face could ruin a whole week of junior high (not that the weeks without a blotch were that good anyway). Growing up, we often learned painful lessons about body image, self-confidence, and the cruel nature of junior high students. My friend Don was a bit of a rebel and shaved his head in high school, much to the shock of his classmates. I always admired his willingness to take risks. I'm afraid his independent spirit, mixed with a little bad judgment, got him into some serious trouble a little later down the line. The last time I saw him, his hairline had completely slipped backward, and his years of wild living had taken a tremendous toll on his health.

When my grandma was in the nursing home, I stopped by one day to see her. It was mid-day, and the dining room was full of residents enjoying an informal activity. As I scanned the room, all I could see was elderly ladies with various shades of gray and white hair. I started to approach one resident then realized it was not Grandma. Not sure where to look, I turned and bumped into an aid wheeling another lady into the room. With a look of embarrassment, I gave up and asked, "Katy?" The aid pointed me in the direction of Grandma's table, and I was relieved to be released from my position of ignorance in the middle of the room.

As I reflected on the embarrassing moment on the way home, the thought occurred to me that Grandma would probably leave this world in the same way that Don and I entered it. Her last days would be spent in a room full of wrinkled strangers, dependent on others to meet their most basic personal needs. I decided that maybe God intends for the aging process to take away all vanity—all concern about what we look like—so that we can focus not on what our hair or clothes look like but on enjoying the relationships that took us a lifetime to build.

Despite all the plastic surgery and all the "fountain of youth" gimmicks, age is the great equalizer. The most beautiful creatures in society will eventually grow old. Wrinkles will happen and hairlines will fade. Hopefully we will have built such lasting and enjoyable relationships that these things are the least of our concerns.

At the senior campus where I work, we have a joke that makes light of the great equalizer. Whenever someone is foolish enough to ask another employee what the new lady looks like, we respond in unison, "She is short, with gray hair and glasses." I hope we still think it's as funny when we're standing around all short, in our gray hair and glasses.

Simple truth: If we took every minute we've spent worrying about how much we weigh, whether we are having a good hair day or bad hair day, or whether our pants make our butt look fat and spent it addressing the needs of others, what a wonderful world this would be!

Never Order Biggies

Have you ever explained something so clearly that you felt there was no possible way for the listener to misunderstand? Maybe you gingerly explained your intentions to a co-worker you just offended, and still she stomped away mad. Or perhaps you have shared an after-work plan with a spouse, only to find him waiting nervously at the back door, wondering why you weren't home on time. I don't think people deliberately misconstrue the message. I just believe there is more than a fair amount of selective listening going on these days.

When my son was in third grade, we sent lunch money with him for a field trip. That evening, we asked him how the field trip went and where they had eaten lunch. He advised that they had eaten at a fast food restaurant and recounted his "biggie" lunch selections. This sounded to us like a tad bit more food than the $5 we gave him might have covered. When asked if he had enough money, he advised that he had to borrow a nickel off the teacher to get an ice cream cone. His father and I launched into a tirade about how he should not have bumped his selections to "biggie" size if he wanted to have enough money for an ice cream cone.

We thought we had properly shamed our son into understanding that tough choices had to be made when you have a limited budget. The argument seemed clear to us. Don't buy more lunch than your budget will cover. Don't ever borrow money off the teacher for such frivolities as ice cream, etc., etc. The crux of our message was to live within your means.

A year after the field trip, we took the kids out to see both sets of grandparents who wintered in Arizona. We left them with my husband's parents and when we met up with the kids a few days later, Grandma and Grandpa inquired as to why Ted was not allowed to have biggies. When he had placed his order and the employee asked Ted if he wanted to make it a biggie, he responded, "My parents told me I should never order biggies." Another teaching moment gone awry.

Wives always think husbands aren't listening when they talk. Parents think their kids aren't listening when they talk. When the kids were young, my husband would say to them, "It's like I talk and nobody listens." But Ted proved us wrong. He was listening—he just didn't get it. Ironically, he's turned out to be very good at handling his money anyway, despite his biggie struggles to stay on budget.

Simple truth: Live within your means, for when it comes time to pay the piper, your third grade teacher probably won't be there to bail you out.

Making It Up on the Road

I have a terrible habit of waiting until the very last minute (and then five minutes more) before I leave for my destination. I almost never allow for even the slightest distraction along the way. I always figure I can make it up on the road.

One beautiful summer day, I left my office to run errands on my 45-minute lunch break. I had my trip mapped out. First stop was the courthouse, where I would change over a vehicle title. Realistically, that task alone could have eaten up my entire lunch break. But I had loftier goals. First the courthouse, then on to the grocery store to pick up a few items for dinner, followed by a quick stop at the post office to buy a book of stamps. And of course I would need to drive through a fast food drive-through to pick up some lunch.

I pulled out of the parking lot and on to the city's main drag. As I approached the first stoplight, I could see traffic backed up farther than usual. I pulled in behind the last car in the right lane and waited for traffic to move. A few minutes passed, and still no movement. I rolled down the window and turned off my car's air conditioner. As I alternated between glaring at the clock on the dashboard and my wristwatch, I grew more nervous with each passing minute. I had no hope of running the lunch race successfully if these morons wouldn't get out of my way!

FISHING IN ROSE-COLORED GLASSES

About five minutes into the waiting game, I become convinced that the stoplight ahead was stuck and the drivers going my direction were simply too dim-witted to take their rightful places in the intersection. As I watched my lunch plans go down the drain, I allowed frustration to wash over me and did something I had not done before and have not done since. I laid on the horn.

In some ways, I suppose I saw that honk as a payback for every time I had fought the urge in a slow-moving fast food line, or for time spent standing in a 20-minute line to return a $5 item, or waiting for a little old guy to finish washing his precious pick-up truck and clear out of the car wash stall. Still, the instant I did it, I knew it was sick and wrong. As I gave an embarrassed shrug to the young mother and daughter in the minivan to my left, the mother gently whacked me between the eyes with an invisible two-by-four: "It's a funeral procession."

I can't remember when I have been so ashamed of myself. The funeral of a young man killed in an auto accident had become a complete annoyance to me, as I rushed selfishly around, taking care of what in an instant went from an all-consuming mission to absolutely meaningless tasks. I said a short prayer for the grief-stricken family and thanked God it was not a friend or a loved one of mine.

I relayed the incident to my psychiatrist boss, who, despite my sense of shame, found great amusement in my embarrassment. He was a patient, gentle soul, who had often times respectfully rebuked me for my tendencies to take on too much and stress myself out. He wrote me a poem that helped me gain some perspective on this shameful situation. It went something like this:

Life got you down? Motorists get in your way? Honk at a dead man, it'll brighten your day.

In a rush to buy groceries? To mail a letter? Honk at a dead man, it'll make you feel better.

No time to sit still? To wait at a light? Honk at a dead man, with all of your might.

Honk at a dead man; honk at the cars. Better be careful, they'll put you behind bars!

Simple truth: Life should not feel like a series of hurried errands and tasks. It should feel like one small but grand adventure after another.

The Anatomy of a Bad Day

A few years back, I experienced what most people would consider the classic "bad day." And I'm not talking about a bad hair day. This was the kind of day when you wake up with a headache and things just keep getting worse. Imagine trying to stay alert and attentive in an educational session on Medicaid when your head is throbbing to the point that you can see your temples moving out of the corners of your eyes. Not that Medicaid is not a fascinating topic, but the combination of the headache and the lack of sleep the previous night had rendered me almost unconscious as I tried to make it through until the next useless dose of Motrin.

When I left home with my headache that morning, I had purposely picked out a lavender suit, hoping it would lift my spirits, if not eradicate my headache. Had I known I would be seen by passersby on the side of the interstate, looking like a neon sign, standing beside my broken-down car, I would have certainly chosen navy or black. Luckily the tow truck driver had a towel to cover the greasy passenger seat. I hopped in the truck, high-heeled shoes in hand, and headed back to the office a mile away and an hour and a half after I had first set out for home. A one-hour commute had just turned into a two-and-a-half-hour commute, topped off by a $250 auto repair bill. And the multiple doses of Motrin had never really kicked in, making this probably the worst day I had experienced in years.

When my daughter was very young, she would overreact to even the slightest bit of trouble. She would come in the house squalling over such major traumas as a kitty scratch or a harsh word spoken by her little brother or the ornery neighbor boy. I would try very hard to help her put this terrible tragedy into perspective and would frequently ask her such questions as, "What if your arm fell off?" Or "What if your mom or dad died?" I was often chastised by family members for using this psychological shock and awe strategy on my daughter, but I simply could find no other way to put a kitty scratch into perspective for her.

The "things could always be worse" theory has always helped me put things in perspective. I called my daughter later that evening to talk about my interstate breakdown and my long, miserable commute home. I admitted to her that just a few days earlier I had been noticing a lot of cars broken down along the road and had marveled that, although I had been driving for 27 years, I had never had a breakdown along the road.

I began to reflect on the day's events with the "things could always be worse" perspective in mind. The breakdown occurred on the interstate, very close to a new exit ramp that had not yet been opened to the public. I was well-protected from traffic and had plenty of room to open my car door and enjoy a beautiful breeze blowing across the interstate. I had a cell phone to call a tow truck and to call my neighbor to warn her that I wasn't going to make church choir practice that evening.

As I pondered the events of my bad day further, I couldn't help but think of my mother-in-law, who at that time was suffering from a terrible disease that had robbed her of the ability to do almost everything she loved. What she wouldn't have given for the opportunity to be behind the wheel of a car, even one that was broken down. She would have loved to be able to hop up in a tow truck, even if wearing a lavender dress. She would have loved to be able to speak loud enough to have a conversation with the tow truck driver over the roar of the engine. Participating in any of these events I considered bothersome would have been a glorious day for her.

It's easy to focus on all that goes wrong in a day—much harder to focus on all that is right and all the blessings we have. The next time you're on your way to an important meeting and you find yourself standing alongside the road with a broken-down car, in the rain, without an umbrella, with a cell phone with a dead battery, wearing a chartreuse suit, wondering how long you will have to stand there until someone stops to help, try asking yourself, "What if my arm fell off?" I think you'll find your problems are very small in comparison.

Simple truth: No matter how many problems we have, there is always somebody who has it worse. Taking a moment to count your blessings instead of cursing your bad luck can help put things into perspective.

The Skelders Are Back

Anyone who lives in the Midwest would have no problem conjuring up a mental picture of the box elder bug. He's a little black and red creature that appears in late summer and converges on country homes in droves. Our family has had a long-term relationship with the box elder bug. One fall, the popular bugs made their yearly convergence on our home. My daughter was fascinated by the clingy little pests. Although she could speak plainly and in full sentences at 18 months, she just could not master the word "box elder."

One day when the box elders were out in full force, my mother-in-law came by for a visit. My daughter inquired, "Grammy, did you know the skelders were here?" Grandma guessed she didn't know the skelders. Were they relatives on the other side of the family? Were they friends of the family? Were they a new religious denomination dropping off some literature? It took Grandma a bit of detective work to determine that the skelders were not any sort of human visitor but the black and red bugs hanging in sheets on the outside of the house.

Grandma discussed with her young granddaughter the evils of the skelder and demonstrated how she killed them by squishing them between her fingers. My daughter was impressed and repulsed all at the same time.

Shortly after being introduced to the "skelder," Grammy developed an incurable disease that eventually robbed her of the ability to do even the simplest of tasks. One late summer day, she spied a bug across the room. Because her voice was weak, her pleas to have the invader dealt with went unheaded. With quiet determination, she mustered every bit of control she could find, pressed the knob on her electric wheelchair, and to the amazement of everyone in the room, made it all the way over to the other side of the room. "There," she whispered, after running back and forth over the visiting skelter a time or two with her wheels. Another skelder bites the dust.

Simple truth: Sometimes, when there's dirty job to be done, you can't sit around and wait for someone else to take care of the problem. You have to take matters into your own hands.

The Right Mix of Force & Reason

Don't you just love reading the instructional signs people post to help you understand what comes next? I especially like signs written for employees but available for all to see. There's nothing like a good sign to let us know what sort of troubles the organization might be facing.

I especially like restaurant signs:

"Employees: Don't forget to wash your hands before returning to work."

It's always nice to be tipped off to the fact that at least a few of the employees preparing your food might be engaging in some unsafe infection control practices. I always wondered many people who don't have the good sense to know to wash their hands would be compelled to follow the instructions on a sign.

"Employees: Please don't forget to wash the utensils after each use."

Translation: Hey, we've got some cross contamination issues in the kitchen."

"Employees: Please do not pick your nose over the salad bar."

I think this one speaks for itself. And thanks for giving me a visual image that will forever turn me off to an otherwise healthy dietary selection.

And then there are the instructional signs aimed at the general public. These are a couple of signs I spotted in a laundromat:

"Do not wash dog diapers."
Are you kidding? Are people really bringing dog diapers to the laundromat? Most people don't even use cloth diapers for their kids!

"Use significant force (within reason) to push handle in and out."
This little gem was posted on the front of the laundry soap dispenser. I had trouble with this one, because I've never had to gauge whether my force is reasonable or unreasonable. And I was afraid if my force turned out to be unreasonable, I might be found upside down, with my dress over my head, on the dirty floor of a laundromat. That's a lot of pressure just to get soap to wash my doggie diapers.

And I like construction-type signs too:

"Do not follow into work area."
This is my favorite truck sign. I have always been amazed to think that people would mindlessly follow a gravel truck off the highway and into a construction zone. Apparently someone has done so at one time or another, or we wouldn't have to see that on every orange construction truck on the road.

And bumper stickers are fun too:
"Keep honking...I'm reloading."
This is my all-time favorite bumper sticker, even though in this age of road-ragers opening fire on other travelers, I probably shouldn't laugh. But it's

kind of a good reminder that you don't really know how the person ahead of you is going to be affected by your obnoxious behaviors. As discussed in the "Honk at a Dead Man," chapter, you don't usually even know what you're honking at!

I think I'll start keeping track of how many organizations have trouble with women flushing unmentionables, people not turning out the lights when they leave the room, and who is not wiping their feet before they enter a room. Maybe I can start a consulting firm that helps people figure out a better way to solve these problems than posting signs that nobody is reading.

Simple truth: If we want to let someone know that they're doing something against the rules or just plain irritating, why not tell them directly? Why air our dirty laundry with a sign that's going to be ignored?

People Who Live in Tipped Houses

Sunday dinner was a tradition in my husband's family. My daughter, who was the long-awaited first grandchild on her father's side of the family, provided the afternoon entertainment just by being her two-year-old self in the middle of the living room while the family watched and laughed.

One Sunday, she began whirling and spinning wildly to watch her "flippy skirt" twirl as the family laughed with delight. Grandma began to worry that her precious granddaughter was going to fall down. "Be careful, Sissy, you're going to get hurt," Grandma warned. About that time, the tiny dancer fell to the floor in a heap. As Grandpa held Grandma back from scooping up the baby, my daughter staggered to her feet, scanned the room, and with a voice of great concern for all onlookers, shouted, "Look out guys. I tipped the house."

I've spent a few tippy days of my own, as an inner ear issue flares up every time I paint a ceiling. My Grandma explained her hip fracture as feeling like the floor had tipped. I don't know if it's just the women in my family or if every family has members living in tipped houses. Whether the tipping is for pure entertainment, a wake-up call that you're not as young as you used to be, or a life-changing event that results in a move to the nursing home, one thing is for sure. Life is not predictable. Just when we think things are going smoothly, we can encounter a house tipping that reminds us of the fragility of the human body and the great and often unrecognized blessing that an ordinary, un-tippy day can be.

Simple truth: Life is full of twists and turns, bumps and thumps, and ups and downs. It's how we handle them that reveals the depth of our character.

When "I Do" Means Forever

When I worked for a long-term care trade association, I had the privilege of being introduced to a couple who had been married for 82 years. Harvey and Leta were gracious enough to agree to be interviewed. The topic for discussion was pretty obvious. In the face of sky-rocketing divorce rates, how can a marriage possibly survive for over 80 years?

Before this interview, I had never had a conversation with someone older than 100 years. As we headed down the hallway, the employee who would introduce me to the couple assured me that Harvey was very "with it" and would be able to answer my questions, but Leta would not be able to communicate, due to a stroke that had taken her voice. As I entered the room, Harvey lay in the prone position on his bed with his eyes shut. My instinct was to turn around and just let him rest, but the employee assured me he loves company and would be disappointed if he knew he missed an opportunity to visit.

As the caregiver placed another pillow under his head, I shook Harvey's hand and introduced myself. Leta sat quietly in a wheelchair beside the bed, with her hands folded atop a lap afghan that she had crocheted many years ago.

As I pelted Harvey with questions on the meaning of life

and his philosophy on marriage, it quickly became apparent that he was a man of great faith. He often referred to the "Lord's plan," to explain such mysteries as why he has lived to be 102, how his marriage had survived 82 years, and why his wife is now unable to walk or speak. Though she remained silent throughout the visit, I could see tears well up in in Leta's eyes as her husband told me what a good cook she was and how clean she kept the house.

Harvey spoke with amazing clarity about those who resided in the nursing home with him, advising me that a couple just down the hall had also been married a long time. In most circles a 64-year marriage would seem incredible, but in this place, 82 years was the brass ring of marital longevity. But I took the story tip he had offered and interviewed Ida and Roy Jones, asking how they had managed to stay married so long and why they believe so many marriages today fail. There were some common themes beginning to emerge between the two interviews.

"I think people get in too deep financially," Ida informed me. "And then they start to take the pressure of that debt out on each other." She told me of how they had started out with used furniture and appliances and never bought anything they couldn't afford. She also advised that many marriages have problems because "everyone wants to be the boss." She recounted how she and Roy had worked together to build a farm and a family. "He took care of the farm, and I took care of the house and garden," she said proudly. We exchanged farm stories about butchering chickens, gathering eggs and canning. And then Ida provided me with yet another tip on another couple that had been married more than 60 years.

My visit with Ellie Brown turned out to be two stories in one. Ellie had been on both sides of the employee/resident balance in the nursing home. As we visited about raising a family and letting go of the child-rearing years gracefully, she told me that after her children left, she "needed something to do." So she applied for a job as a certified nurse aide at a nursing home in a neighboring town and spent seven years caring for seniors. Her husband, who had recently moved from their double room to his own room in the memory care unit, didn't mind that his wife worked every other weekend. After all, Ellie would "leave Dad a little something in the kettle to warm up for supper" when she went off to work at the nursing home. She told me she would have worked several more years if her husband had not fallen ill and required her help.

As I spoke with a member from each of these three farm couples, all of whom had been married more than 60 years, I began to notice some similar guiding principles which seemed to account for the success of these marriages. I sensed that their relationships had survived because they clearly understood and valued the contribution their spouse made to the marriage and the family. There was so much work to be accomplished that there was little time left for arguing about who would take out the garbage. And there was no bickering about whether they should buy a new couch, because they simply waited until they had saved enough money to pay cash.

Another common thread seemed to be that each partner had clearly defined roles, and each one supported and valued the work of their spouse. The focus on building a marriage, a family, and a home left little time to entertain the "what's in this for me?" philosophy that tears so many modern marriages to pieces. All three couples started out with nothing and worked for everything they had. There was no regret, bitterness, or even one thought about who worked harder, but rather a sense of pride in what they had built together. It was apparent that all three couples placed a high value on hard work, commitment, family, neighbors and community.

The couples acknowledged that life is different now, and that in most marriages both people seem to have to work outside the home to "make a go of it" financially. We marveled at how technology created to make life easier has actually complicated life, marriage and raising a family. As I listened to stories of working beside neighbors to build a barn, celebrate birthdays, can the bounty of summer, and church ladies making quilts for the needy, I had a sad sense wash over me that I was born 50 years too late.

Simple truth:
Harvey summed up all we really need to know about marriage. "We didn't want to be apart, and so we got married. That's the Lord's plan and purpose—that we should get married and stay married." Too bad we've lost track of that simple truth.